BRITISH RAILWAYS STEAMING THROUGH PETERBOROUGH

Compiled by

PETER HANDS & COLIN RICHARDS

DEFIANT PUBLICATIONS
190 Yoxall Road
Shirley, Solihull
West Midlands

Printed in the United Kingdom by Netherwood Dalton & Co. Ltd., Huddersfield, England.

CURRENT STEAM PHOTOGRAPH ALBUMS AVAILABLE
FROM DEFIANT PUBLICATIONS

VOLUME 3
A4 size - Hardback. 100 pages
-182 b/w photographs.
£7.95 + 75p postage.
ISBN 0 946857 02 4.

VOLUME 4
A4 size - Hardback. 100 pages
-182 b/w photographs.
£7.95 + 75p postage.
ISBN 0 946857 04 0.

VOLUME 5
A4 size - Hardback. 100 pages
-180 b/w photographs.
£7.95 + 75p postage.
ISBN 0 946857 06 7.

VOLUME 6
A4 size - Hardback. 100 pages
-182 b/w photographs.
£8.45 + 75p postage.
ISBN 0 946857 08 3.

VOLUME 7
A4 size - Hardback. 100 pages
-182 b/w photographs.
£8.45 + 75p postage.
ISBN 0 946857 10 5.

VOLUME 8
A4 size - Hardback. 100 pages
-181 b/w photographs.
£8.95 + 75p postage.
ISBN 0 946857 14 8.

VOLUME 9
A4 size - Hardback. 100 pages.
-182 b/w photographs.
£9.95 + 75p postage.
ISBN 0 946857 18 0.

VOLUME 10
A4 size - Hardback. 100 pages.
-182 b/w photographs.
£9.95 + 75p postage.
ISBN 0 946857 20 2.

VOLUME 11
A4 size - Hardback. 100 pages
-180 b/w photographs.
£10.95 + 75p postage.
ISBN 0 946857 24 5.

BRITISH RAILWAYS STEAMING THROUGH THE SIXTIES

IN PREPARATION

VOLUME 12

BRITISH RAILWAYS STEAMING ON THE EX-LNER LINES

VOLUME 1
A4 size - Hardback. 100 pages.
-187 b/w photographs.
£9.95 + 75p postage.
ISBN 0 946857 19 9.

BRITISH RAILWAYS STEAMING ON THE EX-LNER LINES

IN PREPARATION

VOLUME 2

CURRENT STEAM PHOTOGRAPH ALBUMS AVAILABLE
FROM DEFIANT PUBLICATIONS

VOLUME 1
A4 size - Hardback. 100 pages
-180 b/w photographs.
£8.95 + 75p postage.
ISBN 0 946857 12 1.

VOLUME 2
A4 size - Hardback. 100 pages
-180 b/w photographs.
£8.95 + 75p postage.
ISBN 0 946857 13 X.

VOLUME 3
A4 size - Hardback. 100 pages
-180 b/w photographs.
£9.95 + 75p postage.
ISBN 0 946857 16 4.

VOLUME 4
A4 size - Hardback. 100 pages
-180 b/w photographs.
£9.95 + 75p postage.
ISBN 0 946857 17 2.

VOLUME 5
A4 size - Hardback. 100 pages
-180 b/w photographs.
£9.95 + 75p postage.
ISBN 0 946857 22 9.

VOLUME 6
A4 size - Hardback. 100 pages
-180 b/w photographs.
£9.95 + 75p postage.
ISBN 0 946857 23 7.

BRITISH RAILWAYS
STEAMING
THROUGH THE
FIFTIES

IN
PREPARATION

VOLUME 7

BRITISH RAILWAYS
STEAMING
THROUGH THE
FIFTIES

IN
PREPARATION

VOLUME 8

VOLUME 1
A4 size - Hardback. 100 pages
-188 b/w photographs.
£7.95 + 75p postage.
ISBN 0 946857 03 2.

VOLUME 2
A4 size - Hardback. 100 pages
-181 b/w photographs.
£8.45 + 75p postage.
ISBN 0 946857 11 3.

VOLUME 3
A4 size - hardback. 100 pages
- 179 b/w photographs.
£10.95 + 75p postage.
ISBN 0 946857 25 3.

IN
PREPARATION
MARCH 1990

CURRENT STEAM PHOTOGRAPH ALBUMS AVAILABLE
FROM DEFIANT PUBLICATIONS

BRITISH RAILWAYS STEAMING ON THE LONDON MIDLAND REGION

VOLUME 1
A4 size - Hardback. 100 pages
-184 b/w photographs.
£7.95 + 75p postage.
ISBN 0 946857 05 9.

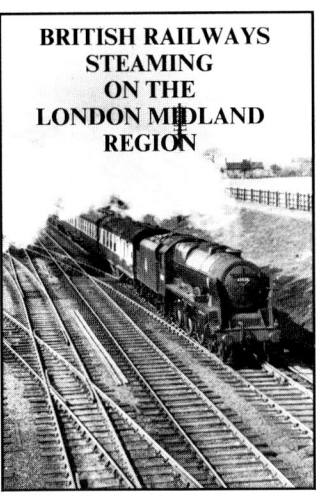

BRITISH RAILWAYS STEAMING ON THE LONDON MIDLAND REGION

VOLUME 2
A4 size - Hardback. 100 pages
-181 b/w photographs.
£8.95 + 75p postage.
ISBN 0 946857 15 6.

BRITISH RAILWAYS STEAMING ON THE LONDON MIDLAND REGION

VOLUME 3
IN
PREPARATION
MARCH 1990

BRITISH RAILWAYS STEAMING ON THE EAST COAST MAIN LINE

A4 size - Hardback. 100 pages
-183 b/w photographs.
£8.95 + 75p postage.
ISBN 0 946857 07 5.
(Reprinted July 1988)

BRITISH RAILWAYS STEAMING ON THE SOUTHERN REGION

VOLUME 1
A4 size - Hardback. 100 pages
-188 b/w photographs.
£8.45 + 75p postage.
ISBN 0 946857 09 1.

BRITISH RAILWAYS STEAMING ON THE SOUTHERN REGION

VOLUME 2
A4 size - Hardback. 100 pages
-181 b/w photographs.
£9.95 + 75p postage.
ISBN 0 946857 21 0.

BRITISH RAILWAYS STEAMING ON THE SOUTHERN REGION

VOLUME 3

BRITISH RAILWAYS STEAMING THROUGH PETERBOROUGH

A4 size - Hardback. 100 pages
-163 b/w photographs.
£10.95 + 75p postage.
ISBN 0 946857 26 1.

OTHER TITLES AVAILABLE FROM DEFIANT PUBLICATIONS
PRICES VARY FROM £1 to £3.80 INCLUDING POSTAGE

WHAT HAPPENED TO STEAM
Volume One
THE GREAT WESTERN
2-8-0's Class 2-8-0's
&
4-6-0 Class 2-8-0's

WHAT HAPPENED TO STEAM

This series of booklets, 50 in all, is designed to inform the reader of the allocations, re-allocations and dates of withdrawal of steam locomotives during their last years of service. From 1957 onwards and finally where the locomotives concerned were stored and subsequently scrapped.

BR STEAM SHED ALLOCATIONS

This series lists all individual steam locomotives based at the different parent depots of B.R. from January 1957 until each depot either closed to steam or closed completely. An attractive bookbinder is available for this thirteen book series.

B.R. STEAM SHED ALLOCATIONS
Part One
WESTERN REGION SHEDS
81A Old Oak Common 81F Oxford
82A Bristol (Bath Road) 82F Weymouth
83A Newton Abbot 83G Penzance

WHAT HAPPENED TO STEAM
THE
L.M.S.
8F 2-8-0's
&
Somerset and Dorset
7F 2-8-0's

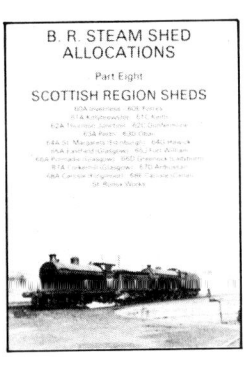

WHAT HAPPENED TO STEAM
THE
L.N.E.R.
B1 4-6-0's.

B.R. STEAM SHED ALLOCATIONS
Part Eight
SCOTTISH REGION SHEDS

B.R. STEAM SHED ALLOCATIONS
Part Seven
NORTH EASTERN REGION SHEDS
53A Hull (Dairycoates) 53E Goole
54A Sunderland 54D Consett
55A Leeds (Holbeck) 55G Huddersfield
56A Wakefield 56G Bradford (Hammerton St.)

CHASING STEAM ON SHED

PETER HANDS

BARBRYN PRESS £5.95 + 50p POSTAGE

ISBN 0 906160 030

This is an account of a locospotters life during the years of 1956-1968. In 1956 when there were 18,000 or so steam locomotives on B.R. it was every locospotters ambition to set eyes on as many locomotives as possible, especially before they were withdrawn.

Every locospotter will remember "shed bashing" trips, some official, mostly unofficial, the challenge they represented and the feeling of delight of having achieved of what was regarded in some cases as the impossible. All these are relived with an almost uncanny accurateness.

We also plot through the various exploits of other railway trips of which there are many positively hilarious accounts and these are backed up most commendably by a series of cartoon illustrations which often capture the mood and atmosphere of those days so perfectly.

Depending on your age, this book will either bring back lots of memories, make you realise what you missed or if you were too young to participate will let you realise what good days they were.

IT'S A DOG'S LIFE
IN THE
FIRE SERVICE

Memories of a 'Happy Squirter'

by

HOSÉ TENDER

A humorous account of life in the Fire Service, complemented by cartoons, spanning in excess of two decades of experiences by the author who was in two separate Fire Brigades which were as different as chalk and cheese and in terms of size went from the sublime to the ridiculous.

Many of the stories related will leave the reader with no doubts that the 'Trumpton's' of the world did exist along with a 'Dad's Army' mentality.

Amongst the chapters, which are described in an amusing manner are: 'Accidents and Breakdowns', 'Open Days', 'Operational Incidents', 'Radio Messages', 'Sickness and Injury', 'Station Drills' and 'Visits from the Hierarchy'.

Although the modern day Fire Service has progressed in leaps and bounds over the years, thanks to technological advances, little has changed in many aspects of day to day iife within the service, especially in the relationships between the officers and the men.

If not available for Christmas 1989
this book will be published during 1990
Order your copy now.

A percentage of the profits from this book will be donated to the Fire Service Benevolent Fund

ACKNOWLEDGEMENTS

Grateful thanks are extended to the following contributors of photographs not only for their use in this book but for their kind patience and long term loan of negatives/ photographs whilst this book was being compiled.

T. R. AMOS
TAMWORTH

H. H. BLEADS
BIRMINGHAM

B. W. L. BROOKSBANK
LONDON

N. L. BROWNE
ALDERSHOT

PETER HAY
HOVE

F. HORNBY
NORTH CHEAM

A. C. INGRAM
WISBECH

H. N. JAMES
IPSWICH

L. PERRIN
BOSTON

N. E. PREEDY
HUCCLECOTE

The two maps on pages 4 and 5 appear with the kind courtesy of Ian Allan Ltd. These are from their excellent publication – 'Rail Centres' – Peterborough – by Peter Waszak. Defiant Publications would like to thank Andrew Farrow and Mike Newcombe for their co-operation in obtaining permission to use the maps.

Front Cover — A magnificent portrait of the north end of Peterborough (North) station, with the splendid cathedral in the background, as photographed from the top of the 'Cenotaph' coaling tower, in 1958. In the right (centre) of the picture is the former GNR North locoshed, which had closed about 1903. It continued in partial use for steam engines, with most normal facilities still available, until it was demolished in the early 1960's. The two locomotives on view are both Thompson B1 Class 4-6-0's Nos 61113 and an ex. works 61207, both from New England shed. Note the 'Extended' water column in the foreground (A. C. Ingram)

ISBN 0 946857 26 1

© P. B. HANDS/C. RICHARDS 1989
FIRST PUBLISHED 1989

INTRODUCTION

BRITISH RAILWAYS STEAMING THROUGH PETERBOROUGH, is the first album to be released by 'Defiant Publications', which concentrates on an individual major railway centre. If this album is a success, it is hoped that similar albums on other railway centres will be released in the future, subject to enough of the right material being available.

The authors hope that the reader will enjoy the splendid photographs within the pages of this album and that many happy memories will be revived for those fortunate enough to visit Peterborough, in steam days. For those that did not, this is an opportunity to see what you missed. The time-scale of this album varies from 22.4.51. to 24.10.64. A large number of prints are from 1957-1958, before the diesels invaded in large numbers.

This album is somewhat unique, as every locomotive which can be identified, even in the background, will only be seen once within the pages of this book. Some 181 engines are portrayed in this manner. A list of the locomotives seen in this book and their relevant page numbers can be seen on page 96. Unless otherwise stated, all locomotives in this book are of former LNER origin.

BRITISH RAILWAYS STEAMING THROUGH PETERBOROUGH is divided into eight chapters, the first five of which cover all types of workings, within, or near to the vicinity of Peterborough (North) station. The majority of the photographs were taken by Messrs. H. R. Cooke and A. V. Fincham, both well known local photographers. These photographs are now the copyright of Andrew Ingram, Wisbech.

The 'BR Steaming' books are designed to give the ordinary, everyday steam photographic enthusiast of the 1950's and 1960's a chance to participate in and give pleasure to others whilst recapturing the twilight days of steam. Wherever possible no famous names will be found. Nevertheless, the content and quality of the majority of photographs selected will be second to none.

The majority of photographs used in these albums have been contributed by readers of Peter Hands series of booklets entitled "What Happened to Steam" & "BR Steam Shed Allocations" and from readers of the earlier "BR Steaming Through the Sixties" albums. In normal circumstances these may have been hidden from the public eye forever.

The continuation of the 'BR Steaming' series etc., depends upon you the reader. If you feel you have suitable material of BR steam locomotives between 1948-1968 and wish to contribute them towards the series and other future publications please contact either:

Peter Hands,
190 Yoxall Road,
Shirley, Solihull,
West Midlands B90 3RN

OR

Colin Richards
28 Kendrick Close,
Damson Parkway, Solihull,
West Midlands B92 0QD

CONTENTS

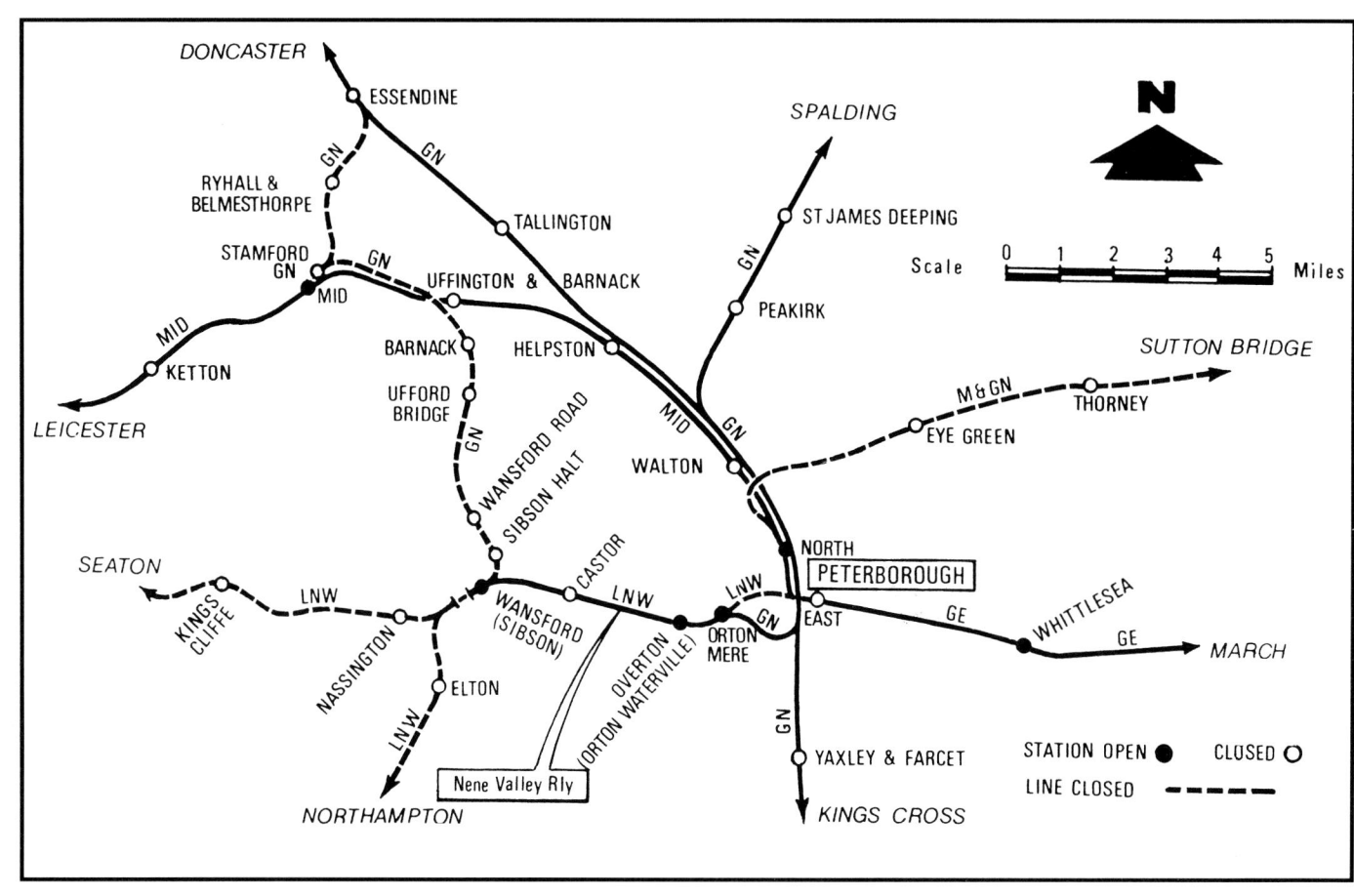

1) Map of the lines and stations in the Peterborough area. (Ian Allan Ltd.)

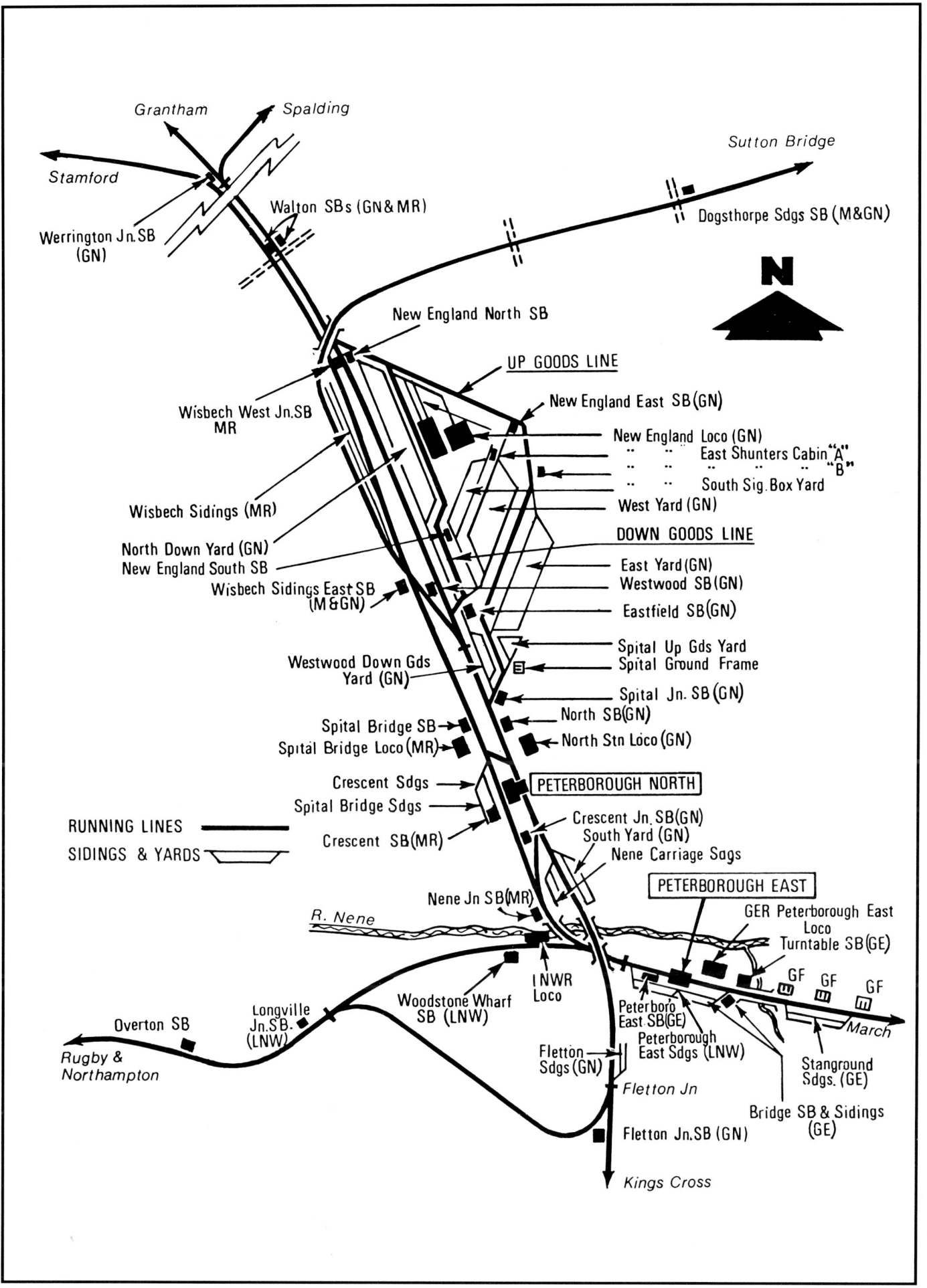

Grantham

Spalding

Stamford

Sutton Bridge

Walton SBs (GN&MR)

Werrington Jn.SB
(GN)

Dogsthorpe Sdgs SB (M&GN)

N

New England North SB

UP GOODS LINE

New England East SB (GN)

Wisbech West Jn.SB
MR

New England Loco (GN)
" " East Shunters Cabin "A"
" " " " " " " "B"
" " South Sig.Box Yard

West Yard (GN)

DOWN GOODS LINE

Wisbech Sidings (MR)

North Down Yard (GN)
New England South SB

East Yard (GN)
Westwood SB (GN)

Wisbech Sidings East SB
(M&GN)

Eastfield SB (GN)

Spital Up Gds Yard
Spital Ground Frame

Westwood Down Gds
Yard (GN)

Spital Jn. SB (GN)

North SB(GN)

Spital Bridge SB
Spital Bridge Loco (MR)

North Stn Loco (GN)

Crescent Sdgs
Spital Bridge Sdgs

PETERBOROUGH NORTH

RUNNING LINES
SIDINGS & YARDS

Crescent SB (MR)

Crescent Jn. SB(GN)
South Yard (GN)
Nene Carriage Sdgs

PETERBOROUGH EAST

GER Peterborough East
Loco
Turntable SB(GE)

R. Nene

Nene Jn SB(MR)

LNWR
Loco

March

Overton SB

Longville
Jn.SB.
(LNW)

Woodstone Wharf
SB (LNW)

Peterboro
East SB(GE)

Peterborough
East Sdgs (LNW)

Stanground
Sdgs. (GE)

Rugby &
Northampton

Fletton
Sdgs (GN)

Bridge SB & Sidings
(GE)

Fletton Jn

Fletton Jn.SB (GN)

Kings Cross

2)   Stations, depots, running lines, yards and signalboxes – Peterborough area – circa 1950. (Ian Allan Ltd.)

3)   An almost deserted interior view of Peterborough (North), looking northwards from Platform 2 to Platform 3 in 1958. Note the treatment meted out to the mailbags in the right foreground. (A. C. Ingram)

4)   A panoramic view of Peterborough (North), taken from beneath Crescent bridge, looking northwards in 1957. A freight train disappears into the distance on the avoiding lines, whilst in the foreground is a mail train being loaded and a parcels van. (A. C. Ingram)

5)   This is a superb panoramic photograph of the northern approaches to Peterborough (North), as viewed from the top of the 'Cenotaph' coaling plant, at Spital Bridge shed in 1958. Several locomotives are to be seen in the left of the picture, including an LMS Class 5 4-6-0. Another engine backs onto the stock in the foreground, as a Gresley V2 Class 2-6-2 sets off with a down express. The coaling plant at New England shed is on the horizon. (A. C. Ingram)

6) A magnificent portrait of Gresley A4 Class 4-6-2 No 60030 *Golden Fleece* (34A Kings Cross) as it stormed out of Peterborough (North) with smoke and steam cascading high into the skies, with a Kings Cross to Newcastle express on Boxing Day, 26th December 1958. *Golden Fleece* had been at Kings Cross shed since September 1957, after a brief sojourn at 35B Grantham. Equipped with a double chimney in May 1958 and paired with a corridor tender, 60030 was withdrawn from 34A in December 1962. (A. C. Ingram)

7) A begrimed Thompson A2/2 Class 4-6-2 No 60504 *Mons Meg* (34E New England) nears the end of its working life as it waited patiently at Peterborough (North) with a down express on 6th August 1960. *Mons Meg*, fitted with miniature smoke deflectors, was rebuilt in 1944 from a Gresley P2 Class 2-8-2. For many years a faithful servant of New England shed, 60504 was withdrawn from there in January 1961. (N. L. Browne)

8) Under clear signals Gresley A3 Class 4-6-2 No 60061 *Pretty Polly* (34A Kings Cross), with small deflectors, passes Peterborough (North) signalbox (G.N.) and glides into the station with an up express bound for Kings Cross on 6th August 1960. *Pretty Polly* had been modified with a double chimney in October 1958 and German smoke deflectors were added in February 1962. The final home for *Pretty Polly* was at 34E New England, from whence it was condemned in September 1963. (F. Hornby)

9

9)   With the Crescent Bridge in the background, Peppercorn A1 Class 4-6-2 No 60133 *Pommern*, from 56C Copley Hill, enveloped in hazy sunshine, passes the South Yard at Peterborough with the up *Queen of Scots*, from Glasgow (Queen Street) to Kings Cross in 1958. *Pommern* was to remain at Copley Hill until the shed closed in September 1964. It was sent to 56B Ardsley, being condemned from there in July 1965. (A. C. Ingram)

10)   A fine panoramic view of Peterborough (North) with a mass of main lines and yards on 16th August 1958. Gresley A3 Class 4-6-2 No 60064 *Tagalie* (36A Doncaster) approaches the camera with a down express. Behind the signal gantry in the right of this picture is an unidentified Gresley 02 Class 2-8-0 on a freight duty. *Tagalie* was withdrawn from service from 34F Grantham in September 1961, having been transferred there in June 1959. (B. W. L. Brooksbank)

11)   34A Kings Cross based Gresley A4 Class 4-6-2 No 60010 *Dominion of Canada* steams under the massive Crescent Bridge and enters Peterborough (North) with the down *Talisman* from Kings Cross to Edinburgh (Waverley) in 1958. Modified with a double chimney in January 1958, 60010 was withdrawn from 61B Aberdeen (Ferryhill) in May 1965. *Dominion of Canada* was restored at Crewe Works during 1966 and 1967 and is now preserved by the Canadian Railroad Historical Association at Montreal. (A. C. Ingram)

12) Gresley A3 Class 4-6-2 No 60062 *Minoru* (34A Kings Cross) sweeps under a pedestrian bridge at Marholm Crossing, to the north of Peterborough, near to Werrington, with a heavy Leeds to Kings Cross express, around May 1959. *Minoru* had received its double chimney in January of this same year and German smoke deflectors were fitted in July 1961. Withdrawal from service came in December 1964, from 34E New England. (A. C. Ingram)

13) With the driver looking forwards from the cab of his charge, Gresley A4 Class 4-6-2 No 60016 *Silver King*, from 52A Gateshead, departs from Peterborough (North) with a down Kings Cross to Newcastle express in 1958. Equipped with a double chimney in June 1957, *Silver King* was one of the members of the class which did not have a corridor tender. Drafted to Scotland in November 1963, 60016 was condemned from 61B Aberdeen (Ferryhill) in March 1965. (A. C. Ingram)

14)   With the driver inspecting the motion and the fireman in charge of the water supplies, Peppercorn A1 Class 4-6-2 No 60117 *Bois Roussel* (56C Copley Hill) takes liquid refreshment at Peterborough (North) whilst in charge of a Leeds to Kings Cross express – circa 1957. Condemned from 56B Ardsley in June 1965, this magnificent beast was reduced to scrap by Clayton and Davie, Dunston-on-Tyne, four months later. (A. C. Ingram)

15)   Sporting an almost brand new double chimney, Gresley A3 Class 4-6-2 No 60108 *Gay Crusader*, a 34A Kings Cross locomotive, heads for home out of Peterborough (North) with an express from Leeds in 1959, consisting of Gresley coaching stock. Despite the fitting of German smoke deflectors in November 1961, this only prolonged the life of *Gay Crusader* for a further two years, with 36A Doncaster being its last home. (A. C. Ingram)

16)   Having blasted the underneath of Crescent Bridge with its sharp exhaust, former Gresley P2 Class 2-8-2, now Thompson
A2/2 Class 4-6-2 No 60506 *Wolf of Badenoch*, a local engine from 34E New England, departs from Peterborough (North)
with an up passenger on a grey and overcast day in 1960. *Wolf of Badenoch*, with small smoke deflectors, had been rebuilt
into a Pacific during 1944. It was condemned in April 1961, from New England and scrapped at Doncaster the following
month. (A. C. Ingram)

17)	With clear signals to the fore and aft, Gresley A3 Class 4-6-2 No 60049 *Galtee More* (34F Grantham) sets off from Peterborough (North) with an express bound for Leeds in 1958. *Galtee More* was to receive a double chimney in March of the following year and German smoke deflectors in October 1960. In company with *Galtee More* is Parker N5 Class 0-6-2T No 69293 (station pilot) and Thompson B1 Class 4-6-0 No 61130 on a local passenger. (A. C. Ingram)

18)	In superb external condition, with a brand new double chimney, ex-works Gresley A4 Class 4-6-2 No 60012 *Commonwealth of Australia*, from 64B Haymarket, leaks steam from its chime whistle on the approach to Peterborough (North) in August 1958. *Commonwealth of Australia* was in charge of an Anglo-Scottish express from Edinburgh (Waverley) to Kings Cross. 60012 was ousted from Haymarket shed when it closed to steam on 9th September 1963. (A. C. Ingram)

19) The final Peppercorn A2 Pacific, No 60539 *Bronzino*, was constructed by British Railways in 1948 and fitted with a double chimney. Based at 52B Heaton, it was poised to depart from Peterborough (North) with a down Kings Cross to Newcastle express in 1959. Surplus to normal express requirements on the ECML in October 1961, *Bronzino* was drafted to 52D Tweedmouth, where it was taken out of revenue earning service twelve months later. (A. C. Ingram)

20) The pride of the LNER was the non-stop *Elizabethan* express from Kings Cross to Edinburgh, which remained in the hands of steam until the diesels took over in 1961. An equally famous train to traverse this route was the *Flying Scotsman*. In charge of the up train on an unspecified date in 1955 was Gresley A4 Class 4-6-2 No 60014 *Silver Link* (34A Kings Cross), complete with the appropriate headboard. *Silver Link* later received a double chimney, in December 1958. (L Perrin)

16

21) A vertical plume of steam erupts from the safety valves of Gresley A3 Class 4-6-2 No 60044 *Melton*, another 34A Kings Cross locomotive, as it heads past a congested South Yard, at Crescent Junction, soon after departing from Peterborough (North) with an up London bound express in 1958. Later modifications to *Melton* came in the shape of a double chimney in October 1959 and German smoke deflectors in August 1961. (A. C. Ingram)

22) Looking in magnificent condition, Peppercorn A1 Class 4-6-2 No 60157 *Great Eastern* (36A Doncaster) beats a path over snow sprinkled tracks as it headed northwards out of Peterborough (North) with a down express in the winter of 1959. Built at Doncaster Works in 1949, *Great Eastern* was one of five members of the class to be fitted with roller bearings. Withdrawal came in January 1965 from Doncaster, after less than sixteen years of service. (A. C. Ingram)

23) Another Peppercorn A1 Class 4-6-2 No 60136 *Alcazar*, again from 36A Doncaster, looks in fine fettle as it sets forth from Peterborough (North) in June 1958, passing a rake of fitted freight wagons with an up Kings Cross express. *Alcazar* was transferred to 34A Kings Cross in August 1958 but returned for a final spell at Doncaster in April 1959, from where its fires were drawn for the last time in May 1963. (A. C. Ingram)

24) Peterborough (North) from a different angle – circa 1959. Gresley A3 Class 4-6-2 No 60059 *Tracery* (34A Kings Cross), fitted with a double chimney in July 1958, blasts a column of black smoke high into the Cambridgeshire sky as it restarted a heavy Kings Cross to Leeds and Bradford express out of the station. Equipped with German smoke deflectors in September 1961, *Tracery* was to survive in service until withdrawn from Kings Cross in December 1962. (A. C. Ingram)

25)   No album on the old London and North Eastern Railway would be complete without the world famous steam record holder, Gresley A4 Class 4-6-2 No 60022 *Mallard*, seen in Peterborough (North) station in 1957, prior to departure with an Edinburgh (Waverley) to Kings cross express. *Mallard*, a longstanding occupant of 34A Kings Cross, had been fitted with a double chimney as long ago as 1938. Withdrawn from 34A in April 1963, *Mallard* is now an important part of the live preservation scene. (A. C. Ingram)

26) Almost obscured by escaping steam, the fireman of Gresley A3 Class 4-6-2 No 60039 *Sandwich*, another engine from the 34A Kings Cross stud, finds his forward view rather restricted, as his charge accelerates out of Platform 2 at Peterborough (North), under Crescent Bridge, with an up London bound express in 1958. Just beyond Crescent Bridge in the right of the picture is Crescent Junction signalbox. (A. C. Ingram)

27) Peppercorn A1 Class 4-6-2 No 60128 *Bongrace* was allocated to 34A Kings Cross from September 1957 until April 1959. It was photographed at Peterborough (North) on a down express to York, in late 1957. To the left of *Bongrace* in the background is an unidentified Gresley V2 Class 2-6-2. After departing from 34A in April 1959, *Bongrace* found itself at 36A Doncaster, from whence it went to a lonely grave in January 1965. (A. C. Ingram)

28) Thompson A2/3 Class 4-6-2 No 60523 *Sun Castle* threads its way between two signal gantries, near to Spital Bridge motive power depot, with an up express in or around April 1958. *Sun Castle*, a 34E New England engine, was re-allocated to 34F Grantham in December 1958. It returned to New England in April 1959, was drafted to 36A Doncaster in January 1960 and came back to New England for the last time in September 1962. (A. C. Ingram)

29) Another of non the corridor tender Gresley A4 Class 4-6-2's was No 60020 *Guillemot*, a 52A Gateshead locomotive. It is seen here arriving at Peterborough (North) with the 10.10 am Kings Cross to Edinburgh (Waverley) express on 31st May 1958, a dull and overcast day. Note the reversed headboard from a named express on the front of this locomotive. *Guillemot* was withdrawn from Gateshead in March 1964 and cut up at Darlington Works four months later. (F. Hornby)

30) The 'one-off' former *Hush-Hush* locomotive, Gresley W Class 4-6-4 No 60700 (36A Doncaster), in less than clean external condition, trundles over the Nene Bridge with a heavy down express in 1958. This ill fated engine, which was withdrawn from Doncaster in June 1959, was the subject of a nasty derailment at Westwood Bridge, Peterborough in September 1955, caused by a fractured bogie frame. (A. C. Ingram)

31)   With a snow-laden sky in the background, a 40B Immingham based Thompson B1 Class 4-6-0 No 61082 ushers an up
        express out of Peterborough (North), near to snow covered sidings at Crescent Junction, in the winter of 1959. Looking
        at the external condition of 61082, one would imagine it had just emerged from Doncaster Works after overhaul. 61082
        was taken out of service from Immingham in December 1962 and disposed of by Cashmores, Great Bridge in July 1963.
        (A. C. Ingram)

32) Gresley B17/6 Class 4-6-0 No 61651 *Derby County* (31A Cambridge), in the twilight of its career, approaches Peterborough (North) in 1959 with an express from Cambridge. *Derby County* had been transferred to Cambridge shed from 30E Colchester in January 1959 and it was condemned in August of the same year, being cut up at Doncaster Works the following month. (A. C. Ingram)

33) With the driver and fireman looking at the photographer, prior to their locomotive taking on fresh water supplies, their charge, Thompson B1 Class 4-6-0 No 61190, from 40B Immingham, sizzled and steamed in Peterborough (North) on a Cleethorpes to Kings Cross express in 1957. 61190 departed from Immingham for pastures new, at 41D Canklow, in January 1965. One final transfer took it to 40E Colwick in June 1965, where it was withdrawn the same month. (A. C. Ingram)

34) Locomotives from the London Midland Region were a common sight within the near vicinity of Peterborough (North), with the former Midland Railway main line running alongside the East Coast Main Line. LMS Stanier Class 5 4-6-0 No 45105, from 26A Newton Heath, was captured by the camera, with train M971, by Westwood Bridge, to the north of Peterborough (North) station, on an up Midland line express – circa 1958. (A. C. Ingram)

35) The prototype Gresley V2 Class 2-6-2 No 60800 *Green Arrow* (34A Kings Cross), heads southwards past Crescent Junction signalbox, under clear signals, with an express for Kings Cross in 1957. Crescent Junction signalbox controlled the southern approaches to the North station until modernisation came along in 1965. *Green Arrow*, withdrawn in August 1962, *like Mallard*, is actively preserved. (A. C. Ingram)

36) Peterborough (North) hosted a stream of titled expresses in steam days. One of the lesser known ones was the *Butlins Express*, which ran during the summer months to and from Skegness. 34A Kings Cross based Thompson B1 Class 4-6-0 No 61075 entered the station with the down train, bound for the seaside resort in July 1959. This engine ended its days at 41F Mexborough, being withdrawn from there in September 1963. (L. Perrin)

37) With a fresh fall of snow on the ground, LMS Stanier Class 5 4-6-0 No 44809, in ex.works condition from 9E Trafford Park, passes under the less imposing part of the Crescent Bridge and Peterborough (North) station with an up express M956, bound for Peterborough (East) during 1958. Once transferred away from Trafford Park in May 1963, 44809 was to serve from many depots, prior to withdrawal from 10A Carnforth, in August 1968. (A. C. Ingram)

38) Probably substituting for a failed Pacific, Gresley V2 Class 2-6-2 No 60903 (34A Kings cross) proudly carries the headboard of the up *Flying Scotsman* as it approaches Peterborough (North) on 1st October 1955. 60903 was re-allocated to 34E New England in December 1962 but only remained in service for a further two months, being condemned in February 1963. It was scrapped at Doncaster Works three months later (L. Perrin)

39) The use of LMS Class 4F 0-6-0's on express duties to and from Peterborough (East) suggests that the motive power authorities on the London Midland routes also had problems with the supply of engines of the appropriate power classifications. On 6th August 1960 a filthy 'Duck 6' was employed on an express from the Midlands to the East Coast. No 44169 (17A Derby) was passing Peterborough (North). (F. Hornby)

40) With the East Coast Main Line in the right of the picture, LMS Hughes Class 6P5F 2-6-0 No 42818 (17B Burton), fitted with Reidinger rotary poppet valve gear, speeds towards the camera at Walton, between Helpston and Peterborough, on the former Midland line, with the 9.55 am express from Derby to Yarmouth (Vauxhall) on 15th August 1959. 42818 was withdrawn from Burton in May 1962 and cut up at Horwich Works the same month. (B. W. L. Brooksbank)

41) 40B Immingham based Thompson B1 Class 4-6-0 No 61079 steams into Peterborough, close to Spital Bridge shed, with a lengthy Cleethorpes to Kings Cross express in 1958. During 1958, Immingham had no less than twenty-four B1's, these being Nos 61079/82/98. 61130/42/43/44/59/68/75/90/95. 61281/84. 61318/25/28/66/74/79/90. 61406/8/9. 61079 was withdrawn from the depot in June 1962 and scrapped at Doncaster a month later. (A. C. Ingram)

42)   The road ahead is clear for this double-header – circa 1959. A far from home LMS Class 5 4-6-0 No 45032, from 8A Edge Hill (Liverpool), pilots an unidentified LMS Class 4F 0-6-0 past Spital Bridge signalbox, close to the depot, with a Peterborough (East) to Leicester train. From January 1957 until condemnation in February 1964, 45032 only worked from three other sheds – 8B Warrington, Edge Hill and finally 8C Speke Junction. (A. C. Ingram)

43)   Freight engine power is once again being employed in this photograph of LMS Class 4F 0-6-0 No 44571, a 21A Saltley engine, as it passed Crescent station with an up express in 1960. Crescent station, once owned by the Midland Railway, had closed as early as August 1866. Before being taken out of service in December 1964, 44571 served at 5B Crewe (South) – twice and 5D Stoke. (A. C. Ingram)

CHAPTER THREE – LOCAL PASSENGER TRAINS

44) With two huge power station chimneys dominating the background, Gresley V2 Class 2-6-2 No 60820, from 34A Kings Cross, passes a caution signal near to Crescent Junction signalbox and readies itself for the stop at Peterborough (North) with a down local in 1958. This locomotive found itself based at 34E New England from September 1959 until it became surplus to requirements in June 1962. It was cut up at Doncaster Works a month later. (A. C. Ingram)

45)　15C Leicester (Midland) based Fowler Class 4 2-6-4T No 42330, in fine external condition, shows a clean pair of heels on the former Midland line at Crescent Junction with a Leicester (Midland) to Peterborough (East) local on a sunny day in 1958. Condemned from Leicester (Midland) in December 1961, its life was ended at Derby Works in February 1962. (A. C. Ingram)

46)　A crowded scene at Peterborough (North) in 1959. Ex. works Gresley A4 Class 4-6-2 No 60006 *Sir Ralph Wedgwood* (34A Kings Cross) provides super power for a down local, probably a running in turn. *Sir Ralph Wedgwood*, equipped with a double chimney in September 1957 did not have the facility of a corridor tender. Its working life was extended in October 1963 when it went to the Scottish Region, being withdrawn in September 1965. (L. Perrin)

47) Nearing the end of its working days, LMS Fowler 'Compound' Class 4P 4-4-0 No 41062, from 21B Bournville, in Birmingham, passes the old Midland Crescent station in Peterborough with a four coach local bound for the East station in 1958. Withdrawn from 17A Derby in May 1959, 41062 languished in store at Spondon Junction, Derby until September 1960, being scrapped at Wards, Woodville, near Burton the following month. (A. C. Ingram)

48) LMS *Jubilee* Class 4-6-0's were rare visitors to Peterborough. The driver of No 45615 *Malay States*, based at 15C Leicester (Midland), takes things easy as his mount emerges from under Crescent Bridge and passes Crescent Junction signalbox on the last stage of the journey from Leicester (Midland) to Peterborough (East) in the summer of 1960. There was only a limited life ahead for *Malay States* with condemnation looming in December 1962. (A. C. Ingram)

49)　A common feature of the 40B Immingham based Thompson B1 Class 4-6-0's was that the majority had their smokebox hinges and numberplate smartened up by a coat of white paint. This has been applied to No 61143, despite the rest of the engine being in a disgraceful condition. 61143 was setting off from Peterborough (North) with a lengthy down stopper from Kings Cross to Cleethorpes in 1958. (A. C. Ingram)

50)　Intermixed with the ex. LMS and LNER locomotives which dominated the railways around Peterborough, BR standard engines also appeared from time to time. BR Class 4 4-6-0 No 75059, a 15C Leicester (Midland) product, was captured by the camera at Crescent Junction with a four coach local for Peterborough (East) in 1958. 75059, introduced into service in April of the previous year, only had a life span of some ten years. (A. C. Ingram)

51)   Yet another 15C Leicester (Midland) engine, this time in the shape of an elderly LMS Fowler Class 2P 4-4-0 No 40452, passes Spital Bridge signalbox with a local from Leicester (Midland) to Peterborough (East) in 1958. The semi-open cab of these engines would have been fine during the summer months but during the winter would have provided spartan cover for the footplate crews. 40452 was condemned from 15C in January 1961. (A. C. Ingram)

52)   In direct contrast to the above locomotive, the modern Ivatt Class 2-6-0's, introduced in 1946, almost provided all the comforts of home. No 46466, from 31A Cambridge, in pristine condition, approaches the camera after passing Crescent Junction signalbox with a stopping train from the East Midlands to Peterborough (East), again during 1958. Despite having youth on its side, 46466 was taken out of service in September 1962, from 31B March. (A. C. Ingram)

53) We take our leave of the passenger services in and around Peterborough (North) with this shot of BR Caprotti Class 5 4-6-0 No 73142, allocated to 15C Leicester (Midland), seen here clearing the cylinder cocks in Platform 6 of the North station – circa 1958. 73142 was about to depart with a Peterborough (East) to Leicester (Midland) train. After departure from 15C in January 1959, 73142 served at 17A Derby (twice), 17C Rowsley and 9H Patricroft before being condemned in May 1968. (A. C. Ingram)

CHAPTER FOUR – FREIGHT TRAFFIC

54) Under the watchful eye of a stationary shunter (complete with pole), BR Class 9F 2-10-0 No 92178, in a soot-stained condition, from 34E New England, storms southwards past Crescent Junction signalbox with an up fitted freight, probably bound for Ferme Park – circa 1963. 92178, equipped with a double chimney, had been allocated to New England from brand new in September 1958. Drafted to 41J Langwith Junction in January 1965, it was withdrawn from there nine months later. (A. C. Ingram)

55) 40E Colwick based Thompson B1 Class 4-6-0 No 61177 skirts the fringes of New England shed with an extremely lengthy partially fitted up freight in 1958. In the right of the picture is the massive concrete water tower, built in 1939, which belonged to the depot. 61177 was taken out of service from Colwick in September 1963 and after a period of storage at the same shed it was despatched to Cashmores, Great Bridge for scrapping. (A. C. Ingram)

56) Ex. Great Eastern Railway Holden J17 Class 0-6-0 No 65584 (31D South Lynn) descends the bank from the Midland & Great Northern Rhubarb Bridge, Peterborough, after shunting the Eye Green Brickyards in 1958. The wagons in the sidings below 65584 create a 'piggy-back' illusion. 65584 was drafted to 31B March in October of the same year and thence to 31C Kings Lynn in November 1959 where the end came in February 1960. (A. C. Ingram)

57) With a wisp of steam issuing from the safety valves, Gresley J6 Class 2P3F 0-6-0 No 64265, a local engine from 34E New England, emerges from under a road bridge and passes Spital Junction signalbox (G.N) with a down partially fitted freight in 1958. These locomotives, first introduced in 1911 were employed in the main on freight and shunting duties and the class was rendered extinct in June 1962. (A. C. Ingram)

58) 'Duck Sixes' in tandem – circa 1959. LMS Class 4F 0-6-0 No 44156 (15D Coalville) and an unidentified sister engine, snake their lengthy Class 8 loose-coupled freight train towards the camera at Nene Junction, to the south of Peterborough (North) station. 44156 went to 15A Wellingborough in January 1960 but returned to Coalville in December 1962. A final transfer took it to 15C Kettering in February 1964. It was condemned the same month. (A. C. Ingram)

59) One of the erstwhile Gresley V2 Class 2-6-2's No 60862 (34A Kings Cross), its cab door flapping outwards, takes a passing loop line at Peterborough (North) with an up fitted freight consisting of a mixture of stock including a cattle truck, in 1958. 60862 remained at Kings Cross until April 1963 when it was re-allocated to 34E New England. Its life was terminated at New England two months later. Note the outside steampipes. (A. C. Ingram)

60) An almost brand new BR Class 9F 2-10-0 No 92144 (35A New England), skirts Nene carriage sidings with a down cattle train in late 1957. Along with many other aspects of British Railways, cattle trains have long disappeared from the everyday scene. 92144 had been put into service at New England in August 1957 and in later life was to work from 40B Immingham, have a second spell at New England, followed by 41J Langwith Junction and 40E Colwick. (A. C. Ingram)

61) An immaculate 34A Kings Cross based Gresley V2 Class 2-6-2 No 60814, in lined black livery, passes through Peterborough (North), with caution, at the head of an up fitted freight in which cattle trucks are once again to the fore, on a warm, sunny day in 1957. 60814 departed from Kings Cross shed for its final base at 34F Grantham in June 1962, from where it was taken out of service in April 1963 and cut up at Doncaster two months later. (L. Perrin)

62) Although LMS Ivatt 'Flying Pig' Class 4 2-6-0 No 43108 was sporting a 31D South Lynn shedplate in 1958, it was never officially allocated there. Records show that 43108 was based at New England shed from at least January 1957 until February 1959 when it went to 40F Boston. In this photograph it was noted passing Peterborough (North) with an up goods on the former Midland line. (A. C. Ingram)

63)   A brand new BR Class 9F 2-10-0 No 92183 (35A New England) passes a fine array of upper quadrant signals at Westwood Bridge with an immense rake of mineral wagons on the up line, heading towards London in December 1957. 92183, equipped with a double chimney, had a working life of just over eight years from construction to destruction. Withdrawn from 36A Doncaster in April 1966, it was disposed of by W. George, Wath in July 1966. (A. C. Ingram)

64)   Only four BR Class 5 4-6-0's were ever allocated to 34A Kings Cross and this was for only brief periods of time. Nos 73071 and 73157-59 and all had been transferred away by October 1958. One of this quartet No 73158 was photographed on a dull day, in early 1958, passing the South Yard at Peterborough with an up mineral train. In common with sister engines 73157 & 73159, 73158 was drafted to 41A Darnall (Sheffield) in October 1958. (A. C. Ingram)

65) Dwarfed by a large wooden posted upper quadrant signal gantry, Gresley J6 Class 2P3F 0-6-0 No 64254, a local inhabitant of 34E New England, waits, tender-first, to leave New England freight sidings with a trip working in 1959, its last year of service. 64254 was withdrawn from New England in October of this year, being scrapped at Gorton Works during the next month. (A. C. Ingram)

66) Thompson B1 Class 4-6-0 No 61145 (40B Immingham) in disgraceful external condition, plods along at Werrington, on the outskirts of Peterborough, with a Class 8 loose-coupled freight on 12th August 1964. As previously mentioned, the majority of Immingham B1's had their smokebox hinges and numberplates 'bulled' up, but by 1964 this had gone by the board. 61145 moved on to 41D Canklow, from Immingham, in January 1965. (T. R. Amos)

67)   36A Doncaster based Gresley V2 Class 2-6-2 No 60841 trundles over the river Nene via the massive girder bridge with an extremely long down fitted freight bound for the north in 1958. 60841 transferred its allegiances to 34F Grantham in June 1960, departing to 34E New England four months later, followed by a final move back to Doncaster in June 1963, from whence it was condemned in September of the same year. Fitted with outside steampipes in August 1959, 60841 was reduced to scrap at Doncaster Works in November 1963. (A. C. Ingram)

68) Forsaking its normal express passenger duties following overhaul at Doncaster Works, Gresley A4 Class 4-6-2 No 60015 *Quicksilver*, from 34A Kings Cross, passes Nene carriage sidings, with a down express freight in 1958. *Quicksilver*, paired with a corridor tender, had received its double chimney in August 1957. It was withdrawn from Kings Cross shed in April 1963, a few weeks before closure and was cut up at Doncaster four months later. (A. C. Ingram)

69) Looking in fine fettle, Gresley K3 Class 2-6-0 No 61974, allocated to 38A Colwick, leaves the West Yard, Peterborough with an up goods in January 1958. Way in the distance is New England South signalbox. The K3 Class of engines had the power classification of 5P6F and were equally as happy being employed on both passenger and freight duties. 61974 survived in service until July 1962, being condemned from 40B Immingham. (A. C. Ingram)

70) A lofty water tower overlooks some lower quadrant signals as former Robinson Great Central 01 Class 2-8-0 No 63780 (31B March) with a long train of mineral wagons, rattles along on the down Midland line near to Westwood Bridge in 1958. 63780 remained faithful to March right up until its withdrawal in July 1963, having been there since a transfer from 38B Annesley in February 1957. (A. C. Ingram)

71) Another apparently ex.works Pacific seen engaged in the freight haulage business during the summer of 1958. After topping his tender up with water, the driver is comfortably back in his cab, prior to departing northbound with Peppercorn A1 Class 4-6-2 No 60158 *Aberdonian* in charge of a down express goods. *Aberdonian* was despatched to 36A Doncaster in October of the same year, remaining on its books until condemnation in December 1964. (A. C. Ingram)

72) BR Class 9F 2-10-0 No 92034, a 34E New England locomotive, departs from Peterborough (North), and passes Crescent Bridge and Crescent Junction signalbox at the head of a lengthy up Class 8 train of mineral wagons, bound for Finsbury Park on an overcast day in 1958. 92034 went to 36C Frodingham for a spell between January and March 1959, returning to New England, where it remained until June 1963, going to 40B Immingham. (A. C. Ingram)

73) On a bright summer's day in July 1960, Gresley J6 Class 2P3F 0-6-0 No 64206 leaves the south end of the Nene Bridge, Peterborough, with an up ballast train. 64206, still sporting the old *Lion & Wheel* logo on the tender and minus shedplate, had been transferred to 34E New England the previous month, from 34D Hitchin. It was working out its last days of revenue earning service prior to withdrawal in September of the same year. (A. C. Ingram)

74)   The last of the former Midland Railway Fowler Class 4F 0-6-0's, numerically speaking, No 44026 (21A Saltley), about to traverse Marholm Crossing, near Peterborough, with a Leicester to Peterborough goods on a dull day in 1957. Note that the two BEWARE OF TRAINS warning notices, guarding a small allotment by the crossing are both legacies of former rival companies. On the left the Midland Railway and on the right the Great Northern. (A. C. Ingram)

75)   One of the powerful Gresley O2 Class 2-8-0's No 63948, from 35B Grantham, approaches Peterborough (North) with the driver peering at the camera from the window of his cab, with a heavily loaded up iron ore train in 1957. This engine remained at Grantham, the code of which changed to 34F on 1st February 1958, until made surplus to requirements in October 1962. It was scrapped by the Central Wagon Co., Ince, Wigan in December 1963. (A. C. Ingram)

76) The photographers viewpoint is slightly impaired by part of the bridge on which he was balancing on whilst photo-
graphing a down express fitted goods which was swinging across a set of points to the north of Peterborough (North)
on a dull and misty day in 1957. In charge of the goods was an immaculate Gresley V2 Class 2-6-2 No 60902 (34A
Kings Cross). 60902 did not leave 34A until December 1962, going to 34E New England. (A. C. Ingram)

77) Almost enveloped in steam, the fireman of begrimed BR Class 9F 2-10-0 No 92141, from 34E (New England), poses for
the camera as his charge departs from tracks close to Spital Bridge shed, with a down partially fitted freight in 1958. After
being constructed in July 1957, 92141 had been based at 34E, moving on to 36A Doncaster in September 1962. It returned
again to New England in March 1963, remaining there until January 1965. (A. C. Ingram)

78) Another of the powerful Gresley O2 Class 2-8-0's No 63934, allocated to 36A Doncaster, was captured by the camera, near Peterborough (North), this time in charge of a down mineral train in 1957. 63934 remained at Doncaster until October 1960, its services being required at 36E Retford where it worked on until condemned in July 1962. Oblivion arrived for 63934 after the cutter's torch was applied at Doncaster in the same month. (A. C. Ingram)

79) With the driver looking forwards towards the camera and the fireman looking away from the lens, an extremely clean 40B Immingham based Thompson B1 Class 4-6-0 No 61098 reverses a single wagon into a siding at Peterborough (North) sidings in 1958. 61098 was being employed on a Kings cross to Cleethorpes passenger train, of which the wagon had been part of the payload, until detached from the train at Peterborough (North). (A. C. Ingram)

CHAPTER FIVE – PARCELS TRAINS, LIGHT ENGINES AND OTHER MOVEMENTS

80)   A sparkling Thomson B2 'Sandringham' Class 4-6-0 No 61616 *Fallodon* (31A Cambridge), paired with a North Eastern tender, throws steam and smoke into the cold winter air, whilst travelling light engine at a snow-covered Crescent Junction in 1958. Its fine external condition did not help *Fallodon* survive beyond September 1959, being withdrawn from Cambridge and cut up at Stratford Works two months afterwards. (A. C. Ingram)

81) For over thirty years examples of the LNER C12 Class 4-4-2 Tanks were utilised for station pilot duties at Peterborough
(North). No 67365 (35A New England) was doing 'the business' at the station on 3rd April 1956. In January 1957 there
were still six of these engines based at New England, Nos 67357/65/76/79/80/94. No 67398 was added to the list in
February 1957. All were withdrawn by November 1958. (Peter Hay)

82) Steam triumphs over diesel at Nene Junction in 1958. Ex. Great Eastern Railway J17 Class 0-6-0 No 65538, from 31B
March, unceremoniously drags a lifeless multiple unit from Peterborough (East) to Peterborough (North). The diesel was
to have the last laugh when 65538 was condemned from March in April of the following year. Less than a month later
and 65538 ceased to exist in the scrapyard at Stratford Works. (A. C. Ingram)

83) One of the massive ex. Great Central Railway A5 Class 4-6-2 Tanks, No 69814, from 35B Grantham, shunts coaching stock at the head of Nene carriage sidings in 1957. These sidings were situated to the south of Peterborough (North) station. The A5 Tanks were first introduced in 1911 by Robinson and the class was rendered extinct by November 1960. 69814 was withdrawn the same month, from 40E Colwick. (A. C. Ingram)

84) Another former Robinson Great Central Railway engine – 04/6 Class 2-8-0 No 63912, in a rather unkempt condition, drifts past the camera, light engine, beside Westwood Bridge in 1959. 63912, resident to 41J Langwith Junction, had been at this depot since January of the same year following a transfer from 41K Tuxford, which closed in February 1959. 63912 survived in service until December 1962, at Langwith Junction. (A. C. Ingram)

85) Despite being virtually brand new, it had not taken very long for 35A New England based 9F 2-10-0 No 92140 to be reduced to a shabby state of cleanliness. Introduced into service in July 1957, 92140 was photographed passing Crescent Junction signalbox at the head of an up parcels train, around October 1957. This engine only had a working life of less than seven years, serving at two depots. The other being 41J Langwith Junction. (A. C. Ingram)

86) A busy scene at the south end of Peterborough (North) in 1958. In the shadow of Crescent Bridge the engine crew of MSLR Parker N5/2 Class 0-6-2T No 69274 replenish the water tanks in the bay platform, between station pilot duties. 69274, an inhabitant of 34E New England since April of the same year, having been transferred from 6D Chester (Northgate), soldiered on in service at Peterborough until condemned in December 1960. (A. C. Ingram)

87) A plume of smoke is thrown skywards from the chimney of Gresley K3 Class 2-6-0 No 61836, from 40B Immingham, as it steamed into Peterborough (North) with a down parcels train on a wet and generally miserable day in 1958. 61836 was re-allocated to 41F Mexborough in January 1959, moving on to 36A Doncaster in June of the same year. It was withdrawn from Doncaster in February 1960 and scrapped at the works during the same month. (A. C. Ingram)

88) A trio of young trainspotters, one of whom appears to be growing out of his trousers, were busy with their notebooks on Platform 6 at Peterborough (North) in September 1958. Ex. Great Northern Railway Ivatt Class C12 4-4-2T No 67363 (34E New England), carrying express passenger lamps, was shunting stock. This engine had only two further months to live, despite its clean external appearance. (A. C. Ingram)

89) Also sporting an express passenger headcode, was Thompson L1 Class 2-6-4T No 67746, a visitor from 34D Hitchin, photographed light engine in Crescent Sidings, Peterborough in 1959. These engines were first introduced in 1945 and the class was rendered extinct by December 1962. 67746 was condemned in July 1962 after transfers to 34A Kings Cross in September 1960 and 40E Colwick in March 1961. (A. C. Ingram)

90) A soot-stained water tower overshadows BR Class 4 4-6-0 No 75060 (15C Leicester – Midland) as its footplate crew prepared to water their charge at Peterborough North sidings, amidst the winter snows of 1958. 75060 was constructed in the early part of 1957 and placed into service at Leicester (Midland) in April of the same year. In common with most of the BR standard types, its life was a brief one, being withdrawn in April 1967. (A. C. Ingram)

91) Looking in an extremely bedraggled condition, former Great Eastern Railway 'Claud Hamilton' D16 Class 4-4-0 No 62570 (31B March) was travelling light engine at Crescent Junction, opposite the South Yard goods shed, in the summer of 1959. Note the stencilled smokebox number. 62570, prior to June 1959, had been allocated to 32D Yarmouth South Town. It was taken out of service from March in December 1959 and was scrapped at Stratford. (A. C. Ingram)

92) A rather unkempt looking LMS Hughes 'Crab' Class 6P5F 2-6-0 No 42816, from 21A Saltley, drifts past the camera, light engine, near to Peterborough (North) station in 1958. 42816 was drafted to 9G Gorton, in Manchester, in November 1959. It continued to serve from this former Great Central Railway complex until no longer needed in September 1964. Scrapping came at Wards, Broughton Lane, Sheffield in March 1965. (A. C. Ingram)

93) The stock of an express flashes past LMS 'Jinty' Class 3F 0-6-0 No 47458, with a chipped funnel, as it was collecting empty stock from Nene carriage sidings, around July 1957. Although carrying a 35B Grantham shedplate, by now it had been transferred to 35C Spital Bridge and it was a probability that the shed staff had not had the opportunity to swap shedplates. In August of the same year it moved 'up-market' to 35A New England. (A. C. Ingram)

94)   LMS Ivatt 'Flying Pig' Class 4 2-6-0 No 43086 (35A New England) about to burrow under the massive girders of Crescent Bridge, travelling tender-first, light engine from 35C Spital Bridge to Peterborough (East) in October 1957. 43086 left New England in December 1960 and had spells at 31B March (twice), 31A Cambridge and 40A Lincoln before returning home in January 1964, being withdrawn in December of the same year. (A. C. Ingram)

95)   The most famous example of the Gresley A3 Class 4-6-2's No 60103 *Flying Scotsman,* from 34A Kings Cross, with a partially scorched smokebox, in charge of a lengthy parcels train, skirts New England shed and passes an unidentified Gresley 02 Class 2-8-0 in 1959. *Flying Scotsman* had been equipped with a double chimney in January of the same year. It received German smoke deflectors in December 1961 and was withdrawn for preservation in January 1963. (A. C. Ingram)

96) Steam leaks from the cylinders of Gresley K2 Class 2-6-0 No 61773 (38A Colwick) as it attempted to move a rake of empty coaching stock out of Nene carriage sidings in 1957. Note the express headlamps, of different shades, already in place and the stencilled 'Colwick' on the front bufferbeam. 61773 moved to 40F Boston in October 1958, then to 40B Immingham in February 1959, returning to Colwick in September 1960. (A. C. Ingram)

97) Gresley B17/1 'Sandringham' Class 4-6-0 No 61623 *Lambton Castle,* from 31A Cambridge, takes things easy between duties, parked in Peterborough North Sidings in 1958. The B17's, introduced in 1928, had a power classification of 5P4F, whereas the modified Thompson B2 Class, rebuilds of the B17's, were classed as 4MT. *Lambton Castle* was condemned from Cambridge in July 1959 and scrapped at Doncaster Works two months after. (A. C. Ingram)

98)   Devoid of any train identifying lamps of any description, BR Class 9F 2-10-0 No 92041 (34E New England) backs, light engine, on to a four coach passenger train in Platform 6 at the north end of Peterborough (North) station on a sunlit day in 1958. Peppercorn A1 Class 4-6-2 No 60122 *Curlew* (34A Kings Cross) looks on in disgust as it took refreshment in Platform 3, whilst in charge of a down northbound express, from Kings Cross. (A. C. Ingram)

99)   Its tender filled to capacity, Peppercorn A1 Class 4-6-2 No 60114 *W. P. Allen,* allocated to 36A Doncaster, poses for the camera in Peterborough North sidings in late 1957. *W. P. Allen,* constructed by British Railways in 1948, had been at Doncaster since September 1957. It was destined to remain at 36A until taken out of traffic in December 1964, being cut up by Hughes Bolckows Ltd., North Blyth in May 1965. (A. C. Ingram)

100) An immaculate ex. Great Eastern Railway D16/3 Class 'Claud Hamilton' 4-4-0 No 62615 (31B March) stands proudly in Peterborough North sidings on 31st May 1958, despite the fact that condemnation was only five months away. Prior to being allocated to March, in June 1957, 62615 had been at 31A Cambridge for about a month, after being drafted there from 31E Bury St. Edmunds. Built at Stratford in July 1923 it died there in December 1958. (F. Hornby)

101) In contrast to the above picture, a filthy dirty BR Class 5 4-6-0 No 73157, a 17A Derby engine, passes the camera light engine near to Peterborough (North) in 1959. In the right background, in the North sidings, an unidentified Gresley N2 Class 0-6-2T awaits its next duty. Before withdrawal in May 1968, 73157 was allocated to 14D Neasden, 14A Cricklewood, 6A Chester, 1G Woodford Halse, 2B Oxley (Wolverhampton) and 9H Patricroft. (A. C. Ingram)

CHAPTER SIX – NEW ENGLAND MOTIVE POWER DEPOT

102) The original running shed at New England was built by the Great Northern Railway in the mid nineteenth century. Under British Railways the old running shed was demolished and rebuilt as a nine road through shed during 1952-1953. It was coded 35A until 1st February 1958, changing to 34E and was situated some one and a half miles from Peterborough (North), on the Grantham side, to the east of the ECML. This introductory photograph shows Gresley K2 Class 2-6-0 No 61759, with a 40F Boston shedplate, Colwick on the bufferbeam but based at New England, in use as a stationary boiler alongside the shed during 1959. (A. C. Ingram)

103) An impressive line-up at the south end of the running shed, beneath the water gantry in November 1960. From left to right are: Thompson B1 Class 4-6-0 No 61174, Gresley J6 Class 0-6-0 No 64223, WD Class 8F 2-8-0 No 90158, LMS Ivatt Class 4 2-6-0 No 43067 and BR Class 9F 2-10-0 No 92149. All of these engines were residents of New England. The overhead water gantry was capable of delivering 1,200 gallons per minute. (A. C. Ingram)

104) The overhead water gantry as photographed from the other side of the yard during 1958, where Gresley A4 Class 4-6-2 No 60029 *Woodcock* (34A Kings Cross) was to be seen, in company with an unidentified Gresley V2 Class 2-6-2. 60029 was one of eleven members of the class to be transferred to New England upon the closure of 34A Kings Cross on 17th June 1963, the others being Nos 60006-8/10/17/21/25/26/32 & 34. (A. C. Ingram)

105) A decrepit looking Gresley V2 Class 2-6-2 No 60966, a local engine, stands out of steam in the shed yard, near to the ramshackle looking coal stage on 10th April 1960. Hiding in the right background was one of the diesel shunters first introduced in 1955 0-6-0 No D3449. Between January 1957 and June 1963, when the last examples had departed from New England, no less than forty-two V2 Class engines were based here at different times. (F. Hornby)

106) A view of the depot from the north end in June 1959, with the fitting shed on the left and the running shed on the right. On view are a selection of locomotives including two Thompson B1 Class 4-6-0's Nos 61073 and 61272, both New England engines, a WD Class 8F 2-8-0 and a BR Class 9F 2-10-0, numbers not known. 61073 was withdrawn from the shed in September 1963, followed by 61272 in January 1965. (H. H. Bleads)

107) In the immediate vicinity of New England shed there was a massive group of sidings, where Gresley K1 Class 2-6-0 No 62070, the last member of the class and allocated to 31B March, was to be found in April 1959, after being serviced. None of these useful locomotives were based at New England. 62070 moved south to 30A Stratford, in East London in June of the same year, returning to March in September 1961. (A. C. Ingram)

108) A view of the yard, by the water gantry, in the early morning of 31st March 1953. New England hosts a Scottish visitor, Thompson A2/1 Class 4-6-2 No 60510 *Robert the Bruce,* from 64B Haymarket, fitted with an ugly, rimless double chimney. Built at Darlington Works in January 1945, it was re-allocated to 64A St. Margarets (Edinburgh) in July 1960 and condemned four months later, being scrapped at Doncaster in February 1961. (F. Hornby)

109) 34A Kings Cross based Gresley A3 Class 4-6-2 No 60055 *Woolwinder,* moves away from the coaling plant after being refuelled, in the summer of 1958. *Woolwinder* had been fitted with a double chimney in June of the same year. Built in 1925, 60055 carried the original number of 2554 followed later by 55. Being one of the first members of the class to be withdrawn, in September 1961 it never carried German smoke deflectors. (A. C. Ingram)

110) Only eight of the Gresley V2 Class 2-6-2's ever carried nameplates and none of these, at least from January 1957 onwards, were ever allocated to New England. Parted from its tender and dumped in a siding at the shed in 1958 was 52A Gateshead based No 60860 *Durham School.* Transferred to 52B Heaton in January 1960, 60860 was condemned in October 1962 and it was stored in the open at 52C Blaydon prior to scrapping in May 1963. (A. C. Ingram)

111) The most famous members of the Gresley A4 Class 4-6-2's were Nos 60007 *Sir Nigel Gresley,* 60014 *Silver Link* and 60022 *Mallard.* The first member of this auspicious trio, *Sir Nigel Gresley* (34A Kings Cross) was in immaculate external condition in the shed yard after a trial run after overhaul in January 1958, when it received its double chimney. Withdrawn from 61B Aberdeen (Ferryhill) in February 1966, 60007 is now actively preserved. (A. C. Ingram)

112) Like the V2 Class 2-6-2's, only a small proportion of the Thompson B1 Class 4-6-0's were named, a total of fifty-nine. The last, numerically speaking, was No 61379 *Mayflower,* which also carried commemorative plates on the cab, heralding the exploits of the famous ship it was named after. *Mayflower* was captured by the camera in the yard at New England in 1958, whilst visiting the shed from its home base at 40B Immingham. (A. C. Ingram)

113) A gentle jet of steam hisses from the front end of Thompson A2/3 Class 4-6-2 No 60500 *Edward Thompson,* a New England engine, as it shared the ash disposal road with LMS Stanier Class 8F 2-8-0 No 48638, a foreigner from 16A Nottingham on 25th May 1963. *Edward Thompson* was condemned the following month and yet on 5th May 1963 it had been noted in the Crimpsall steam repair bay at Doncaster Works, strange to say the least!!! (N. E. Preedy)

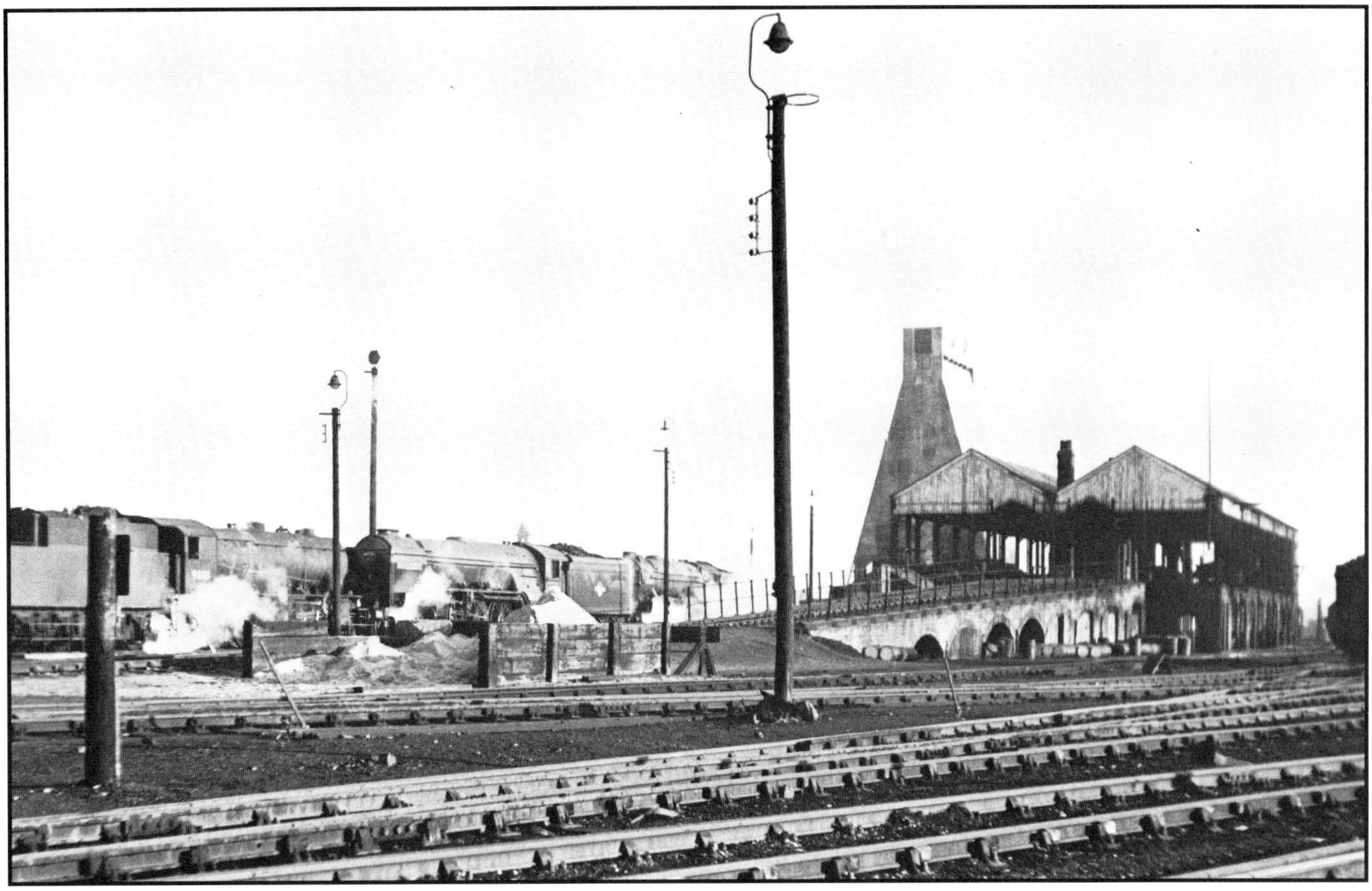

114) The massive concrete automatic coaling plant, constructed in 1932, towers over the ancient coal stage in the right of this picture, taken in 1958. In the left of the picture are a trio of locomotives on the coaling road, these being: WD Class 8F 2-8-0 No 90111, a visitor from 36C Frodingham, which is facing ex. works Thompson A2/3 Class 4-6-2 No 60520 *Owen Tudor,* from 34F Grantham, in company with an unidentified A2/2 engine. (A. C. Ingram)

115) A trio of footplatemen were engaged in conversation by North New England signalbox in 1958. Gresley A4 Class 4-6-2 No 60026 *Miles Beevor* (34A Kings Cross) was coupled to an unknown sister engine prior to leaving the shed. 60026 was drafted to Scotland from 34E in October 1963, along with Nos 60006/7/10 & 34. Of the remainder, Nos 60008/17/21/25/29 & 32, all were withdrawn between July and October 1963, with 60008 being preserved. (A. C. Ingram)

116) Sulphur fumes fill the atmosphere in the shed yard on a late afternoon in 1958. Nearest to the camera is former Great Central Robinson 04/7 Class 2-8-0 No 63634, from 41J Langwith Junction. Facing 63634 are two filthy WD Class 8F 2-8-0's, the first of which is No 90730, a native of New England. 63634 was taken out of service from 40B Immingham in September 1962 and 90730 was condemned from 41E Staveley (Barrow Hill) in October 1965. (A. C. Ingram)

117) LMS Whitelegg Class 3P 4-4-2T No 41949, from 31F Spital Bridge, trespasses on rival territory and shunts coaching stock at 34E, around April 1958, the leading coach of which is of the Gresley origin, in 'blood and custard' livery. 41949, in exemplary condition, moved on to 31B March in August 1959, returned to Spital Bridge two months later and like 'pass the parcel' went back to March in February 1960 where it was withdrawn in April. (A. C. Ingram)

118) With the overhead water gantry in the picture, a simmering 34A Kings Cross based, Thompson B1 Class 4-6-0 No 61331 poses for the camera on a bright sunlit day in 1957. Next to 61331 a tender from an unknown WD Class 8F 2-8-0 protrudes into the picture. 61331 parted company with Kings Cross shed as a home base in March 1960, coming to New England. It was condemned in September 1963 and scrapped at King's, Norwich. (A. C. Ingram)

119) In common with all major depots, New England had its fair share of tank engine classes for use on local passengers, freight trains, station pilots and shunting duties. One of the classes represented, albeit in small numbers, were the GER Holden J69 Class 0-6-0 Tanks. Photographed in the shed yard in 1958, is J69/1 No 68635, fitted with air pumps. 68635 was transferred to 34F Grantham in January 1959. (A. C. Ingram)

120) Fresh from overhaul at Doncaster Works, where it acquired its double chimney, 64B Haymarket based Gresley A3 Class 4-6-2 No 60090 *Grand Parade,* somewhat over-coaled, heads a trio of locomotives at the north end of New England shed in August 1958. *Grand Parade* later had German smoke deflectors fitted, in January 1963. Completing this line-up is a Thompson B1 Class 4-6-0 and a BR Class 9F 2-10-0, both unidentified. (A. C. Ingram)

121) From at least January 1957 onwards, only two former LMS Classes were based at New England, these being a large number of Ivatt 'Flying Pig' Class 4 2-6-0's and smaller numbers of Class 3F 'Jinty' 0-6-0 Tanks. Between January 1957 and January 1965, some thirty-two members of the former class served here, though not all at the same time. One of the regulars, No 43061 was noted in the shed yard on 22nd April 1951. (H. N. James)

122) Having changed a set of points, the driver climbed back into the cab of his charge, a visiting ex. Great Central J11 Class 0-6-0 No 64355, from 40B Immingham, to New England shed during 1957. These engines were first introduced in 1901 and to the author's knowledge none were allocated to New England. 64355 was eventually withdrawn from Immingham in July 1962 and scrapped at Gorton Works four months later. (A. C. Ingram)

123) Only a small number of Gresley A3 Class 4-6-2's were stationed at New England. One of the last to reside here was No 60106 *Flying Fox,* seen in a quite deplorable state, on 24th October 1964, along with an equally atrocious looking 40B Immingham Thompson B1 Class 4-6-0 No 61026 *Ourebi,* next to which was a posing 'winkle-pickered' spotter. *Flying Fox* had been fitted with a double chimney in April 1959 and deflectors in October 1961. (A. C. Ingram)

124) A longstanding locomotive which was based at New England was one of the WD Class 8F 2-8-0's No 90246, seen in abysmal condition in the shed yard on 10th April 1960. Again, referring to records, a total of fifty-nine engines worked at different times from New England, between January 1957 and October 1963, when the last examples Nos 90158, 90246, 90349, 90454 and 90514 were transferred to other depots on the Eastern Region. (N. L. Browne)

125) Agility is an asset when you are working with a saddle tank, as this engineman discovered as he attempted the climb on to Ivatt J52 Class 0-6-0T No 68840, in filthy condition, on a grey day in April 1956, on the ash disposal road. Maybe, older men around the yard of New England, to which 68840 belonged, had given him some advice about getting to the tank filler, without falling off. 68840 was withdrawn in January 1958. (Peter Hay)

126) With the driver at the helm, Peppercorn Pacific A1 Class 4-6-2 No 60116 *Hal O' The Wynd,* a visitor from 52B Heaton, steams past the camera, light engine, in New England yard in 1958. *Hal O' the Wynd* was later despatched to 52D Tweedmouth in September 1962 and ended its days at 52A Gateshead in June 1965, having been drafted there in October 1964. It was stored at 52H Tyne Dock from March to August 1965 before final disposal. (A. C. Ingram)

127) Bright sunshine streams into the south side of New England shed yard in late 1958, where Gresley A3 Class 4-6-2 No 60046 *Diamond Jubilee* (36A Doncaster), fitted with a double chimney in July of the same year, awaited its next duty. German style deflectors were added to 60046 in December 1961, but not for long as it was condemned in June 1963. To the left of *Diamond Jubilee* was a local BR Class 9F 2-10-0 No 92036. (A. C. Ingram)

128) We bid farewell to New England shed, which closed to steam on 4th January 1965, with this final photograph which was taken on the north side of the depot in 1959. Bathed in sunlight are, from left to right: Gresley J50 Class 0-6-0T No 68896 (34E), ex. G.C.R. Robinson 04/8 Class 2-8-0 No 63785 (36E Retford) and LMS Ivatt 'Flying Pig' Class 4 2-6-0 No 43107 (40F Boston). The shed closed forever on 2nd October 1968 and was soon demolished. (A. C. Ingram)

129) A cold looking driver looks towards the camera from the cab of a clean looking Riddles WD Class 8F 2-8-0 No 90528, from 31F Spital Bridge, as it entered Peterborough (East) station in a flurry of white smoke and steam, tender-first, with an up stopping goods train on a snow covered winter's day in 1958. 90528 moved on to 31B March in February 1960 and prior to withdrawal in September 1965, served at 30A Stratford, 36A Doncaster, 36E Retford and finally at 40E Colwick. (A. C. Ingram)

130) A rather less than clean LMS Ivatt 'Flying Pig' Class 4 2-6-0 No 43142, from 31D South Lynn, heads out of Peterborough (East) with a lengthy goods train bound for Leicester during 1957. Ousted from South Lynn shed in February 1959, after closure, 43142 moved on to 40F Boston, remaining there until April 1961, from whence it went to 36E Retford, but the following month it again returned to Boston, being condemned in October 1963. (A. C. Ingram)

131) Having passed Nene Junction signalbox, LMS Fowler Class 4F 0-6-0 No 44247, from 35C Spital Bridge, negotiates the sharp curve which crosses the river Nene, before burrowing under the ECML Nene Bridge and heading for Peterborough (East) with an up passenger working in 1957. 44247 departed from Spital Bridge in February 1960 and went to 2E Northampton. It was withdrawn from 9D Newton Heath in December 1965. (A. C. Ingram)

132) A fine view of the tracks leading under the Nene Bridge, again taken in 1957. 35A New England based LMS Ivatt Class 4 2-6-0 No 43084 approaches the camera after coming off the curved link line from Nene Junction, with a lightweight up freight bound for Peterborough (East) from Leicester. 43084 stayed at New England until July 1964. In the latter years of its life it was on the North Eastern Region, being condemned in September 1967. (A. C. Ingram)

133) The driver looks to the camera as his engine LMS Fowler Class 3F 0-6-0T No 47300 sizzles in Peterborough (East) station, at the head of what appears to be a parcels train, although the engine is carrying an express passenger headcode, in 1958. Spital Bridge had a small batch of these engines but all had been transferred by March 1958, with the exception of 47300 which lingered at the depot until February 1960. (A. C. Ingram)

134) Gresley 'Sandringham' B17/4 Class 4-6-0 No 61657 *Doncaster Rovers,* from 31B March, emerges from beneath the East Coast Main Line and heads towards March with an up express, near Peterborough (East) in 1957. *Doncaster Rovers* was to remain allocated to March shed until rendered redundant by the ever increasing fleet of diesels appearing at the shed, in June 1960, being one of the last active members of this famous class. (A. C. Ingram)

135) Two light engines, harnessed in tandem, pass the camera by the Town Bridge, near to Peterborough (East) in 1958. Nearest to the camera is LMS Fowler Class 4F 0-6-0 No 43885, allocated to 15D Coalville, behind which is an unidentified member of the LMS Ivatt Class 2 2-6-0's. 43885 was drafted to 16B Kirkby in January 1959, where its life was ended in February 1964. It was cut up at Looms, Spondon seven months later. (A. C. Ingram)

136)	With the once Great Eastern owned signalbox (on stilts) and the station in the background, LMS Stanier Class 8F 2-8-0 No 48061, from 15C Leicester (Midlands) sets off from the sidings at Peterborough (East) and heads homewards with a down freight train in 1957. During the intervening years between 1957 and condemnation in September 1967, 48061 was to serve from seven different sheds, the last being 10F Rose Grove. (A. C. Ingram)

137)	We return to the sharp curve between Nene Junction and Peterborough (East), where LMS Class 4F 0-6-0 No 44539 (15D Coalville) had a clear road ahead as it passed a tall, track circuited upper quadrant, showing all clear in the winter of 1958. 44539 was in charge of an up mineral train and in the right of the picture there is a glimpse of Nene carriage sidings. 44539 soldiered on in service at Coalville until condemned in September 1963. (A. C. Ingram)

138) LMS Stanier Class 8F 2-8-0 No 48726, from 3D Aston, steams past the former London & North Western Railway shed, with a LNW line goods train in 1958 and approaches the ex. Midland Railway Junction, Peterborough. The LNWR locoshed, glimpsed behind the wagons, had closed in May 1939 but was still intact over twenty-five years later. In the right of this picture is the spur across the river Nene to Nene Junction. (A. C. Ingram)

139) A smartly turned out LMS Stanier Class 5 4-6-0 No 45288, allocated to 1A Willesden, passes under the Town Bridge and enters Peterborough (East) with an up local passenger train in 1958. 45288 was to remain at Willesden until October 1963, apart from a brief break in October 1960, when it was at 2A Rugby. After October 1963 up and to withdrawal in November 1967, it worked from five different sheds, the final one being 9F Heaton Mersey. (A. C. Ingram)

140) Excursion traffic was very common at Peterborough (East) during the summer months, most being hauled by former LMS locomotives. On a drab July day in 1957, LMS Class 5 4-6-0 No 45308, a 3E Monument Lane engine, departs from Peterborough East, passes the Town Bridge and takes the LNW line to Rugby and then on to Birmingham (New Street) with a down special. 45308 was destined to survive until August 1967, from 5D Stoke. (A. C. Ingram)

141) With steam roaring from the safety valves, LMS Stanier Class 8F 2-8-0 No 48273, stationed at 18A Toton, rattles from beneath the Nene Bridge, at the head of a long up goods train near to Peterborough (East) in 1957. 48273 was transferred to 9E Trafford Park in September 1958, remaining at this Manchester depot for many years, finally bowing to the inevitable in August 1965. Scrapping came at Buttigiegs, Newport in November 1965. (A. C. Ingram)

142) Another West Midlands based engine, LMS Class 5 4-6-0 No 44914, from 3A Bescot, hauls a Yarmouth to Rugby and Birmingham (New Street) special (W317) out of Peterborough (East) in 1958 and passes the outer home signal, complete with its track circuiting sign and indicator board. Examples of this class survived in great numbers into 1967, the last full year of steam on British Railways. 44914 went in August of this year. (A. C. Ingram)

143) Birmingham based locomotives were frequent visitors to Peterborough both on passenger and freight workings. The scenery near to Peterborough (East) is all but blotted out by the smoke issuing from LMS Stanier Class 8F 2-8-0 No 48719 (3D Aston) as it approached the camera with an up Class 8 loose-coupled freight in 1958. This engine was to fall victim to condemnation in August 1965, from 2F Bescot. (A. C. Ingram)

144) LMS Fairburn Class 4 2-6-4T No 42061, from 2A Rugby, emerges from beneath the Town Bridge and heads homewards past the impressive short posted double signal gantry on its way out of Peterborough (East), taking the LNW line, with a down express working in 1957. 42061 remained at Rugby shed until July 1960, transferring its allegiances to 9B Stockport. It was withdrawn from 8M Southport in September 1965. (A. C. Ingram)

145) Gresley B17/6 'Sandringham' Class 4-6-0 No 61633 *Kimbolton Castle* (31B March) passes under the massive girder Nene Bridge and the East Coast Main Line and heads up the link line to Spital Bridge shed, light engine, from LNW Junction, in the background in 1958. The lines to the right lead to Rugby and Northampton. *Kimbolton Castle* remained in service at March shed until no longer required, in September 1959, being cut up the following month at Doncaster. (A. C. Ingram)

146) With the driver looking forwards, with intense concentration on his face, former Midland Railway Class 4F 0-6-0 No 43854, from 15D Coalville, accelerates away from Nene Junction signalbox, having topped the curved gradient from LNW Junction with a down Peterborough (East) to Leicester (Midland) express, in the summer of 1959. This erstwhile servant managed to soldier on at Coalville until condemned in June 1964. (A. C. Ingram)

147) Peterborough (East) station as photographed in 1972, prior to demolition. The line to Northampton had closed to passengers on 2nd May 1964 and to Rugby, via Seaton on 6th June 1966. Peterborough (East) also closed on 6.6.66, by coincidence being one of those unique dates in time. It then became a parcels centre, closing forever in 1972. (A. C. Ingram)

CHAPTER EIGHT – SPITAL BRIDGE
MOTIVE POWER DEPOT

148) This former Midland Railway locoshed was situated almost opposite Peterborough (North) station signalbox across the running lines of the ECML and the MR. It consisted of one large roundhouse and a rather cramped yard. Gathered round the turntable on an unspecified date in 1958 were five engines of LMS origins, from left to right: Ivatt Class 4 2-6-0 No 43127, Whitelegg Class 3P 4-4-2T No 41975, Fowler Class 4F 0-6-0 No 44273 and two Stanier Class 4 2-6-4 Tanks Nos 42541 and 42573 from 2A Rugby. (A. C. Ingram)

149) A view of the depot, looking south-east from the footbridge leading to the shed in 1957. In the foreground, being admired by a relaxed railwayman, is LMS Stanier Class 8F 2-8-0 No 48386 (15A Wellingborough) its tender appearing to consist of little else but slack. In the background are a trio of unidentified LMS Fowler Class 4F 0-6-0's and in the distance is the concrete 'Cenotaph' coaling plant. (A. C. Ingram)

150) Steam amidst the winter snows in the shed yard at Spital Bridge during 1958. Nearest to the camera is a locally based LMS Fowler Class 4F 0-6-0 No 44152 behind which is Gresley J39 Class 0-6-0 No 64789, also from Spital Bridge. 44152 was withdrawn from 31B March in September 1961 and cut up at Horwich Works in March 1962. 64789 demised in July 1960, also from March and was scrapped at Darlington Works the same month. (A. C. Ingram)

151) A dismal and foggy day in 1957, where a visiting LMS Hughes Class 6P5F 2-6-0 No 42824, from 17B Burton, had been serviced and was ready for the road once again, with more than a good supply of coal, to say the least. 42824 was fitted with Reidinger rotary poppet valve gear. It was stored out of service at Burton from March to October 1962, being officially withdrawn in July 1962 and was cut up at Horwich four months later. (A. C. Ingram)

152) Two visiting LMS Stanier Class 8F 2-8-0's grace the shed yard at Spital Bridge in June 1959. The leading one can be identified as No 48314, allocated to 18A Toton. This engine had been a longstanding inmate of Toton and was destined to remain there until August 1965, when it was transferred to 16F Burton, being condemned in December of the same year. Like many a victim before it, 48314 was destroyed by Cashmores of Great Bridge. (H. H. Bleads)

153) What an evocotive photograph this is, with live steam a' plenty on the coaling road, as seen from the 'Cenotaph' plant in 1958. One can almost smell the smoke and feel the heat from the boilers. Visible in this scene is a WD Class 2-8-0 (far left), an LMS Stanier Class 8F 2-8-0, an Ivatt Class 4 'Flying Pig' 2-6-0 and two LMS Fowler Class 4F 0-6-0's, one being a Spital Bridge allocated example, No 44476. This engine was eventually withdrawn from 16A Nottingham in May 1963. (A. C. Ingram)

154) A virtually brand new BR Class 4 2-6-0 No 76086, from 15C Leicester (Midland), simmers under the 'Cenotaph' coaling plant in 1958. This engine was placed into service at 15C in April of the same year. It was drafted to 9E Trafford Park in January 1959 and thereafter it moved to 14A Cricklewood in October 1962. Between then and withdrawal in September 1966, it served at 5D Stoke, 2E Saltley (twice), 2F Bescot, 6F Machynlleth and 6C Croes Newydd. (A. C. Ingram)

155) It was not often one saw locomotives with self-weighing tenders, let alone be in the ideal position to photograph them. Spital Bridge shed possessed one of these 'rare beasts', in the shape of Thompson B1 Class 4-6-0 No 61095, seen in steam over an ash disposal pit in 1958. 61095 had received this particular tender, No 4155, in October 1953 and retained it until withdrawn from 40A Lincoln in December 1963. (A. C. Ingram)

156) LMS Stanier Class 5 4-6-0 No 44690, its exterior stained with muck and filth, visits Spital Bridge from 15C Leicester (Midland) where it was photographed in steam in the shed yard in June 1959. It had been transferred to Leicester (Midland) from 17A Derby in January 1959. It was destined to last to the end of steam, being condemned at 10F Rose Grove in August 1968 and scrapped at Wards, Beighton, Sheffield later in the year. (H. H. Bleads)

157) Another visitor which was photographed at Spital Bridge was LMS Stanier Class 8F 2-8-0 No 48380, allocated to 15B Kettering, coaled and ready for its next duty during 1958. 48380 was a favourite animal at Kettering, not moving on until September 1964, to 15E Coalville. Further transfers between October 1965 and eventual withdrawal in June 1968, took 48380 to 15A Leicester (Midland), 16B Colwick and finally to 9K Bolton. (A. C. Ingram)

158) The engine in this photograph would have been an extremely rare 'cop' for spotters in the Peterborough area in 1958. Seen fresh from overhaul in the yard at Spital Bridge, was LMS Stanier Class 4 2-6-4T No 42445, from far off 27F Brunswick in Liverpool, in company with LMS Fowler Class 4F 0-6-0 No 44388, a more local 'foreigner' from 15F Market Harborough. Following overhaul it is somewhat of a mystery as to why 42445 was at Spital Bridge. (A. C. Ingram)

159) A smartly turned out Gresley B12/3 Class 4-6-0 No 61575, based at 31A Cambridge, takes on fresh water supplies on a misty and cold looking day in 1958, in the yard at Spital Bridge. These engines were originally of Great Eastern Railway origin, being first introduced by Holden in 1911. They were rebuilt, from 1932 onwards by Sir Nigel Gresley. 61575 was almost at the end of its career, with withdrawal on the horizon in April 1959. (A. C. Ingram)

160) A young member of the shed staff at Spital Bridge, uses a lengthy 'pricker' to rake the embers in the firebox of LMS Fowler
      Class 4F 0-6-0 No 44178, from 17E Heaton Mersey in 1957. This splendid close-up clearly shows most of the controls
      on the footplate of 44178. This locomotive was transferred to 18A Toton in June 1958, where it remained until September
      1963, moving on to 18B Westhouses, from whence it was taken out of service in November 1964. (A. C. Ingram)

161) A last look at live steam in the shed yard in October 1959, where LMS Ivatt Class 4 'Flying Pig' 2-6-0 No 43087, from 31C Kings Lynn was taking refreshment. Looking on was another 'stranger in the camp', LMS Ivatt Class 2 2-6-2T No 41227, from 2A Rugby. Within a few months, steam would be nothing more than a memory in the mind's eye of both shed staff and spotters alike. Both 41227 and 43087 were to survive until late 1964. (A. C. Ingram)

162) Under British Railways, Spital Bridge first came under the LMR, having the code of 16B until 1950. From 1950 until closure on 15th February 1960 it belonged to the Eastern Region adopting the code 35C until 1st February 1958. This changed to 31F until the depot died. The allocation consisted of a variety of LMS and LNER classes and a few WD Class 8F 2-8-0's. As photographed on Sunday 20th March 1960 the famous landmark of the 'Cenotaph' coaling plant was being demolished. (A. C. Ingram)

NUMERICAL INDEX OF LOCOMOTIVES